Technology for the elders

Technology For The Elderly.

Tom Carson

Signed By Tom Carson

<2020>

Copyright © <2020> by <Tom Carson>

All rights reserved. This book or any portion thereof may not be reproduced or used in any manner whatsoever without the express written permission of the publisher except for the use of brief quotations in a book review or scholarly journal.

Dedication

To All The Elderly's Out Struggling To Send An Email!

Thank you. Without your support and patience, I would have never achieved my dream.>

.

Contents

Introduction 1

Chapter 1: How To Send An Email ....

Chapter 2: How To Work The Youtube ....

Chapter 3: Whats The Difference By A Computer And A Ipad ....

Chapter 4: How To Send A Text Message.............................

Chapter 5: What Is A Book?...

Chapter 6: Why Apple Is Better The Android ....

Chapter 7: how To Get Ur Child Off The Phone.....................

Chapter 8: The End Speech..

Acknowledgements

I Would Like To Thank My Dad For Saying He Will Help Me But Never Did ☺

<Author Name>

Introduction

This Is Just For The People Who Have No Clue On How To Work A Piece Of The Cool Technology In Our Generation

<A Book by Tom Carson>

<Author Name>

Chapter 1: How To Send An Email

- Follow these step-by-step instructions to send an email
- Step 1: Log in to your Gmail account so that you are on the dashboard (main page) of your mail account.
- Step 2: Click Compose.

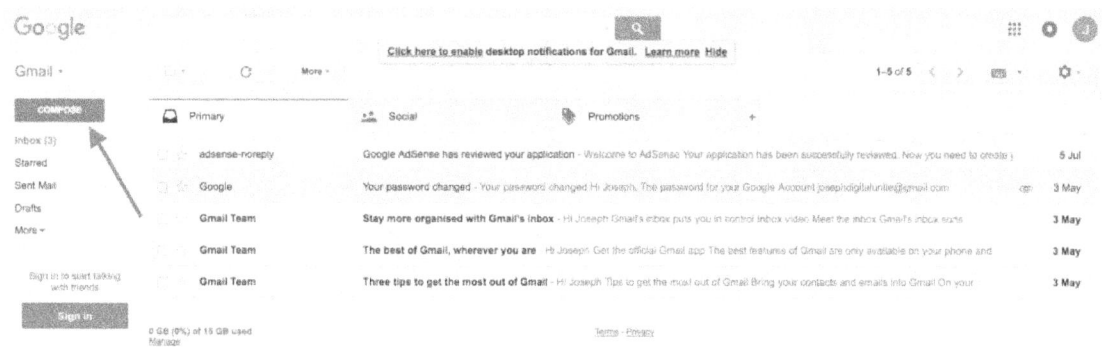

Step 3: A new blank email window will open up. In the 'To' box, type in the email address of the recipient.

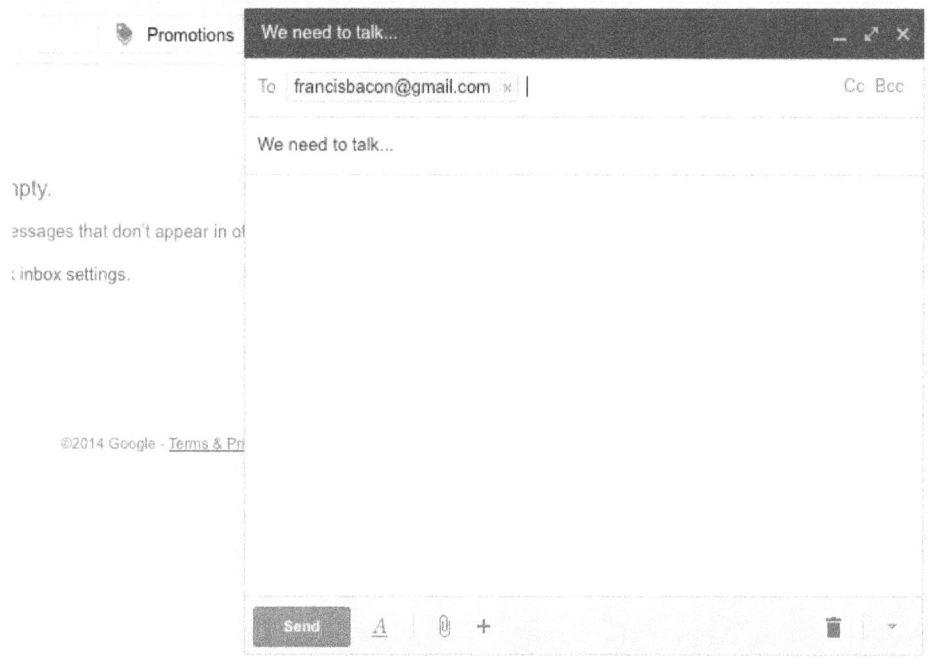

- **Step 4:** You might want to include someone else in your email to 'keep them in the loop'. You can do this by clicking Cc or Bcc, which will open another field. 'Cc' means 'carbon copy' and 'Bcc' means 'blind carbon copy'. Adding an email address to the 'Cc' field means that that person will receive a copy of the email and all the other recipients will see their email address. If an email address is put into the 'Bcc' field, the person will get a copy of the email but no other recipient will see that address.
- If you are sending the same email to lots of different people, it's a good idea to put all the email addresses in the 'Bcc' field to keep your 'mailing list' confidential. That way, there's no chance that it could fall into the hands of a spammer or hacker.

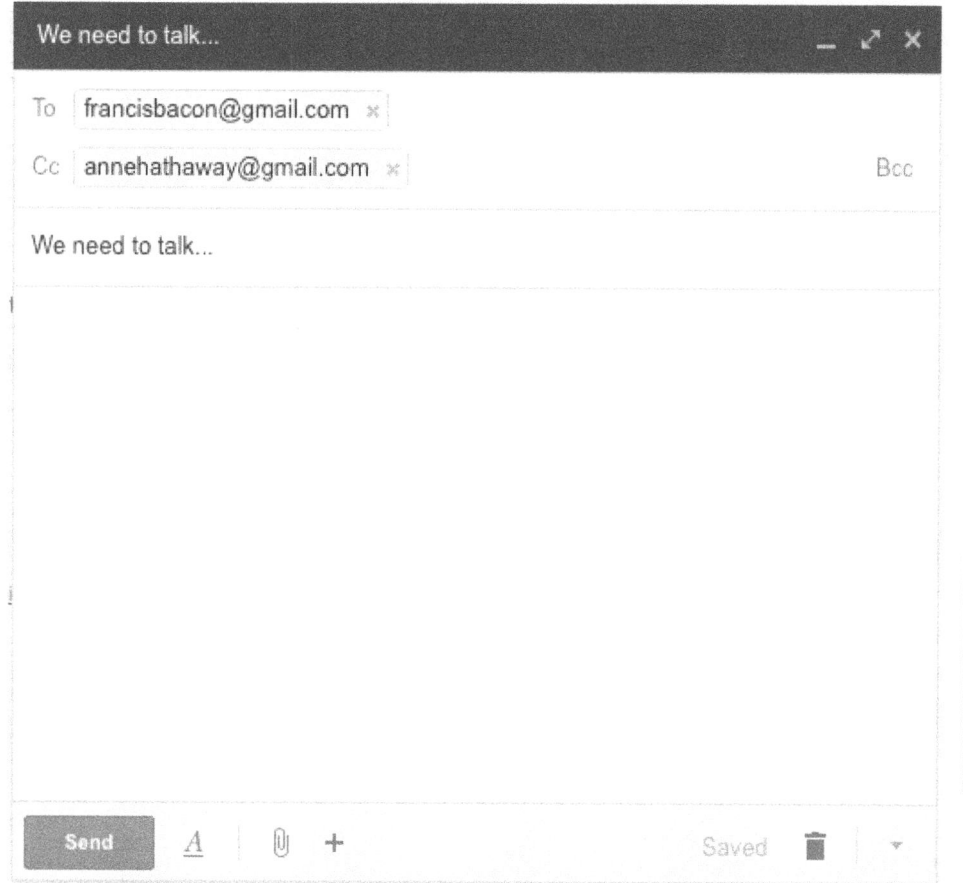

- **Step 5:** The subject field allows you to give the recipient an idea of the topic of your email, like a heading. You don't have to put anything in the subject box, but it can help when viewing and sorting email.
- **Step 6:** Email text can be formatted in a similar way to text in a word document. You can change the font style, colour and size using the formatting icons. You can also create bullet points and check the spelling of your email. Choose your formatting from the menu shown.

Step 7: Type your message in the main body field of your email.

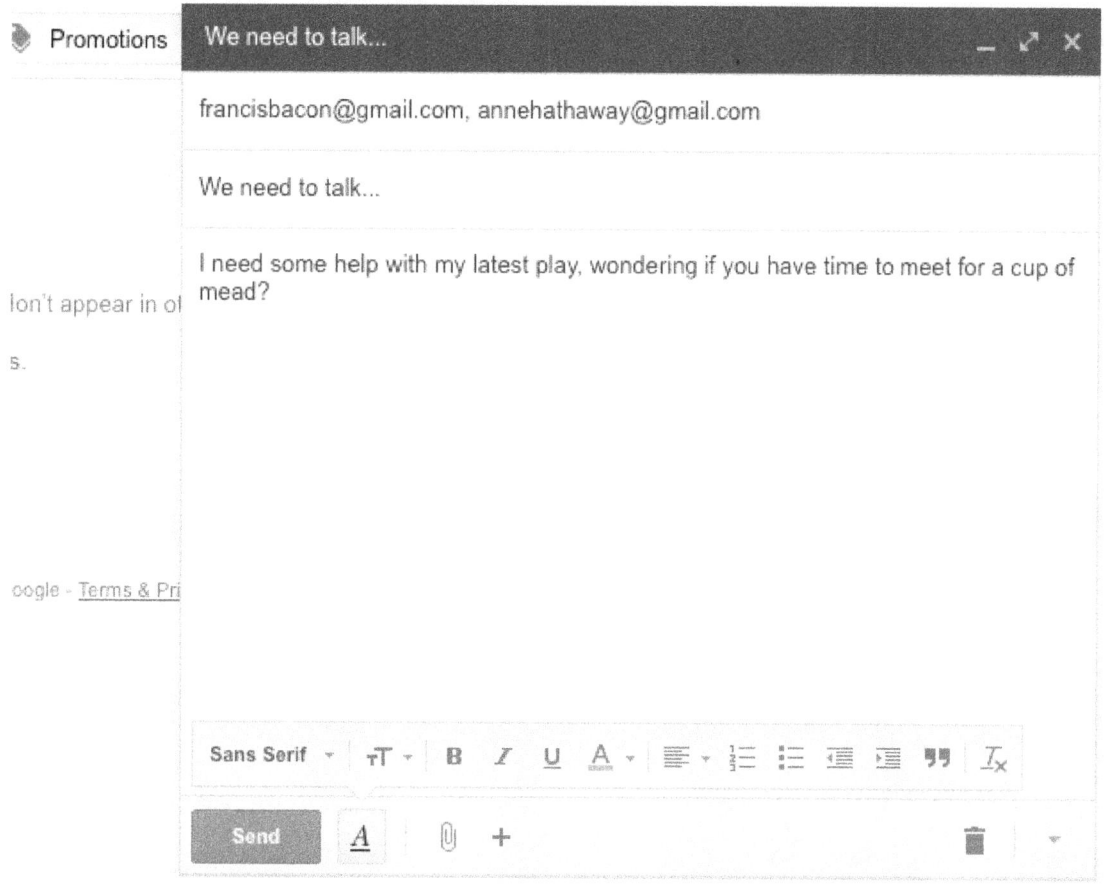

You can format your email using the options that are available on the toolbar. To add a link in the body of your email click on the insert link icon, then add the 'Text to display' and then a web or email address, finally click OK

Step 8: When you're happy with your email, click the blue Send button at the bottom of the compose window.

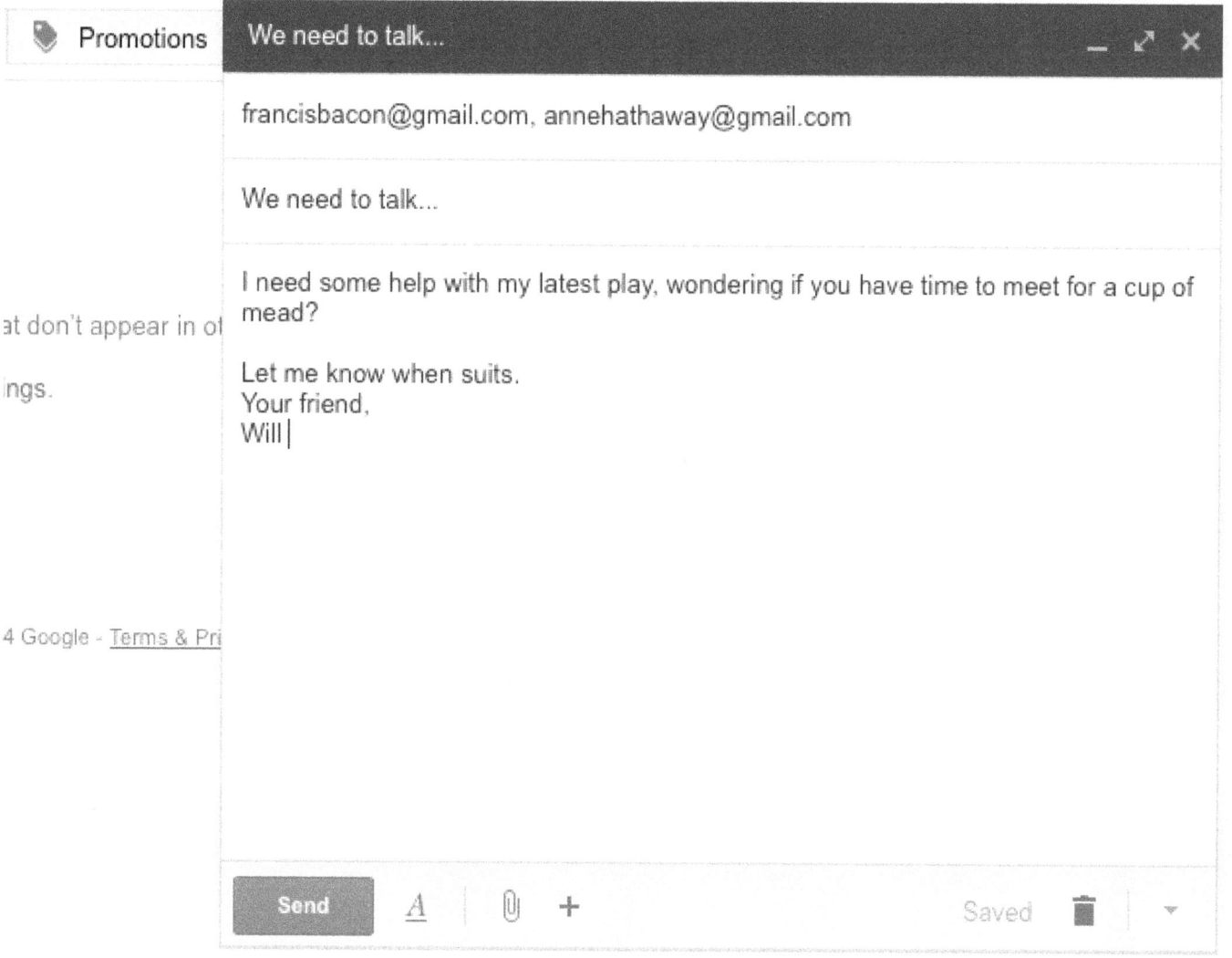

Step 9: The email you've sent will now be stored in the 'Sent Mail' folder on your Gmail dashboard. You may have to run your mouse pointer over the Inbox folder link to see the other folders.

Step 10:

You may start an email but then decide to come back to it later rather than sending it straightaway. Gmail saves your drafts automatically. So you can simply close the email and the unfinished email will be saved to your 'Drafts' folder. When you decide that you're ready to send it, you can retrieve it from the 'Drafts' folder by clicking Drafts and then clicking the correct item in the 'Drafts' folder list. Finish the email

And

Click

Send

As

normal.

Chapter 2: How To Work the Youtube

Since it first launched in 2005, YouTube has quickly become the number one destination for video content online, attracting over one billion regular users. The Google-owned site gained popularity by enabling people to share their videos with others all over the world, whether it's an amusing clip of their pet, or footage of them dancing in their living room.

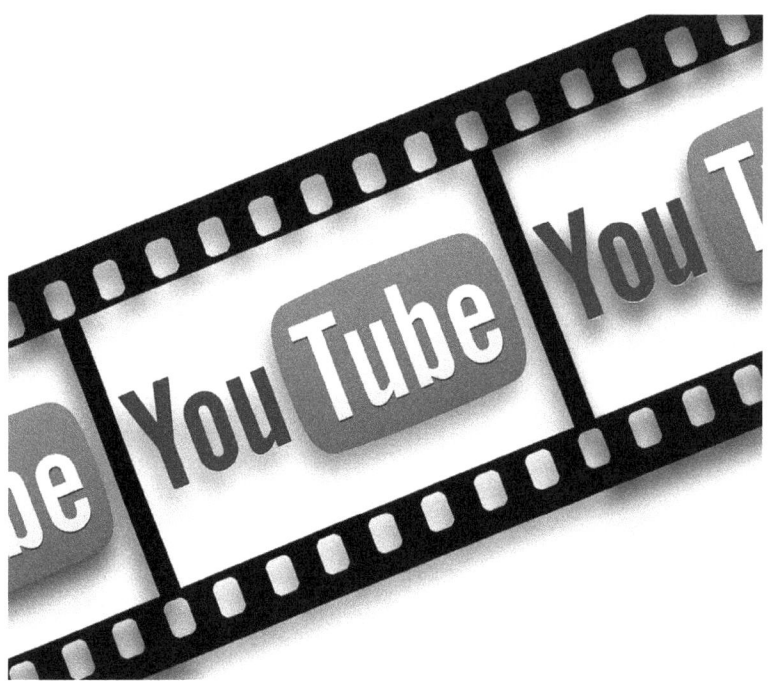

It's not all about cute cat videos and funny home movies though, as YouTube has also helped people launch careers. For example, pop star Justin Bieber was first discovered when a talent scout saw videos of him singing on the site, and Zoe Sugg, aka Zoella, has got her own book deal and range of beauty products as a result of her popular video blog, or 'vlog'. You can even earn money directly from YouTube too, as the site shares some of the revenue it makes from companies who pay to run adverts before or over your video.

The popularity of YouTube is mainly down to how easy the website is to use. Videos in a range of file formats can be uploaded as YouTube converts it into its Adobe Flash video format, with the file extension .FLV, for you. This enables the video to be played using YouTube's Flash player, which can be installed on your computer or smart device for free.

Another benefit of YouTube is the ability to embed videos on other websites. By simply copying and pasting a bit of HTML code, you can enable people to watch a video on your own website using the YouTube player. This saves you having to host the video on your site which requires a lot of bandwidth. Bandwidth is the range of signal frequencies needed to transmit data over the internet and you have to pay for the amount you use. YouTube streams vast amounts of data each day, carrying the bandwidth burden for other sites that want to display vid]

YouTube sensation Zoe Sugg, aka Zoella, films her beauty videos in her bedroom

Going viral
How to become a YouTube celebrity

1 Find your niche
Choose a topic or theme for your YouTube channel that's interesting and or entertaining, and hasn't been done before. For example, YouTube celebrity Zoella gives fashion and beauty tips and reviews her favourite products.

2 Create a studio
You could film your video using your smartphone, but for a more professional look, set up a camera on a tripod. Either make use of the natural light by shooting outdoors or in a well-lit room, or you can set up your own lighting.

3 Upload your video
Finish off your video using editing software, cutting out unnecessary footage and making sure the audio can be heard. Now create a YouTube account and upload your video. The site will automatically convert it into the correct Adobe Flash video format for you.

4 Give it a title
When naming your video, make sure you include any keywords relating to the topic featured and think about what sort of terms people might search for to find it. Also give it an appropriate thumbnail image and a comprehensive description.

Although embedding is great for spreading your videos further across the internet, most people will actually find them simply by searching. To help connect users to the videos they are looking for, YouTube uses a complex algorithm made up of over one million lines of code. When you search for a video, the algorithm decides which search results it will show you and in what order. One of the main factors used to rank the results is video metadata. This is the title, description, thumbnail and tags that you give your video when you upload it, so you should make sure they are relevant to the content of the video and what people might search for to find it. However, the other ranking methods YouTube uses are out of your control. The site used to rank its videos by how many times they had been viewed, but this presented a few problems. It often meant that new videos were pushed to the bottom of the list as their view counts had not yet had a chance to grow, and it also enabled people to manipulate their ranking by clicking on their video repeatedly, as clicking the play icon counts as a view.

<Just For The Elderly>

To combat these problems, YouTube has switched to a new system of measuring a video's quality by the length of time it has been watched for. If several users have stopped watching after a few seconds, this suggests that the video had a misleading title or thumbnail and didn't give viewers what they were looking for, whereas if they stayed to watch until the end it was most likely appropriate for the search terms used and therefore worthy of a high ranking. The rest of YouTube's ranking tricks are a mystery though, as the company is very secretive about its algorithm and changes it all the time to stop people

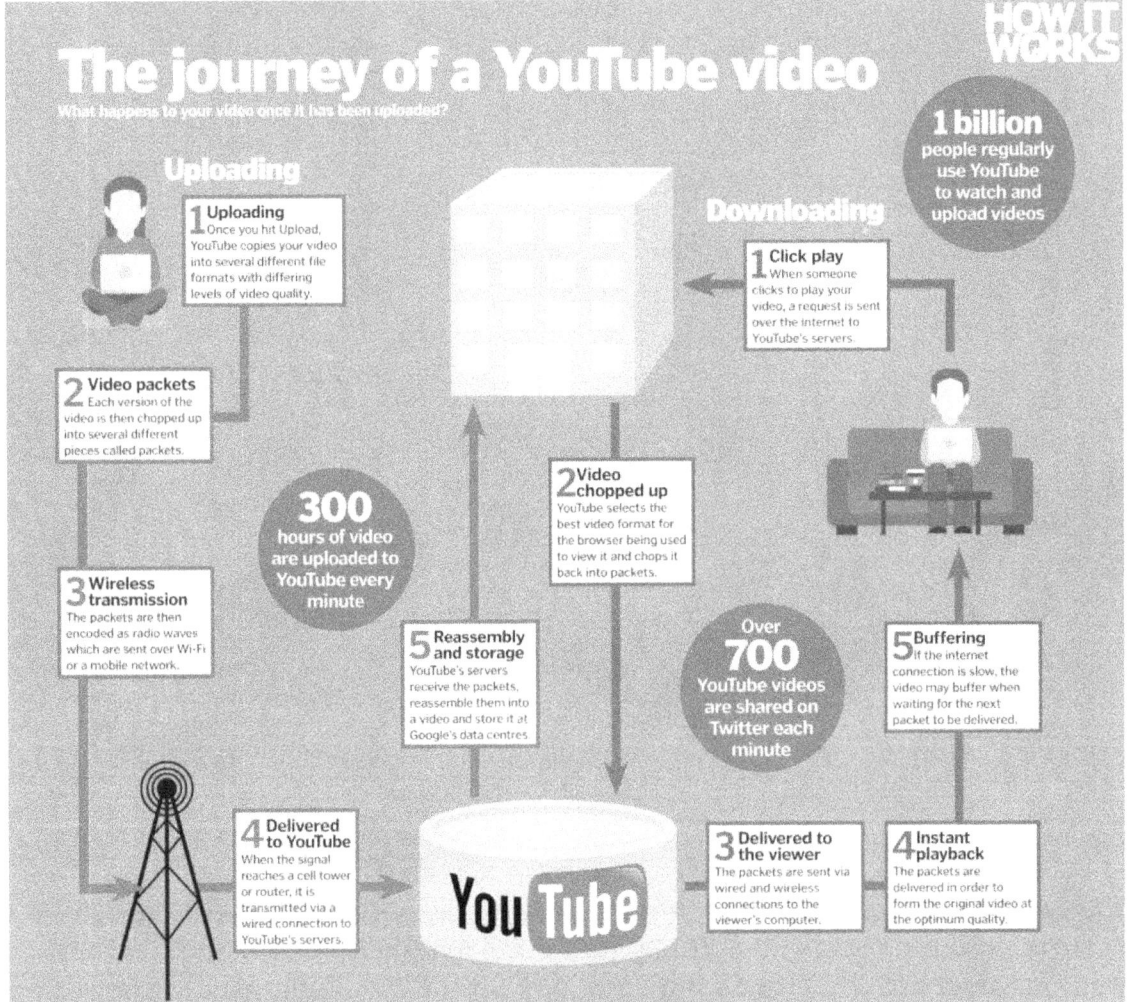

Every video uploaded to YouTube is stored in at least one of Google's 14 data centres spread across the world. These enormous buildings contain thousands of servers – the powerful computers that handle the billions of Google searches made every day and also store your videos. Giant cooling towers keep the temperature inside at a steady 27 degrees Celsius (80 degrees Fahrenheit) to ensure the equipment runs smoothly, and each piece of data is stored on at least two servers for extra security. The data centres can also communicate with each other to send information between them. When you upload your video, it will be stored at the data centre nearest you, but when someone wants to play it, the video will be sent to their nearest data centre for quick access. This also means that in the event of a fire or other disaster, the data is sent to another data centre so that it's always accessible.

<Tom Carson>

Hope

You

Got

That

\<Just For The Elderly\>

Chapter 3: What Is the Difference Between A Ipad And A Computer

Apple iPad vs Laptop

The Apple iPad is a new device in the Apple line-up along with the iPod and the iPhone and it takes on the mobile computing market. Probably the biggest competitor of the iPad is the standard laptop, but unlike the laptop which opens up to reveal the screen and the keyboard, the iPad is a tablet or slate, which does not have any hinges.

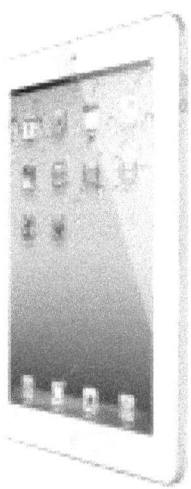

The major contributor to the design of the iPad is the lack of a physical keyboard that takes up a lot of space. Instead, the iPad has a touch screen that is used for all input needs. A software keyboard can appear on screen and you can use that to type anything you want. But for typing out entire documents, a physical keyboard is still much better than the on-screen keyboard of the iPad.

A problem with the iPad is the use of applications. Although there are thousands of applications for the iPad, it is nowhere near that to laptops. You also can't install just any application as there is no way to do that outside of the Apple app store; so you can't create your own program on the iPad and run it. Another software problem is the lack of true multi-tasking. This is a limitation imposed by Apple in order to prevent users from running too many applications and bogging down the iPad.

Aside from software issues, there are also several hardware limitations to the iPad. First, its battery is built-in to the device and is not user replaceable. This means you can't have spare batteries and you need to look for an outlet every time you run out of charge. You also do not have the option to upgrade any part or even use external storage like memory cards or flash drives. The only way to upgrade the iPad is to get a newer one in case they release one. Although upgrade options for laptops are pretty limited, it is existent.

It's becoming harder and harder to decide between an iPad and a laptop or a desktop PC. The original iPad was a mobile device aimed directly at the netbook. And it demolished them. The iPad has become a more capable device each year, and with the iPad Pro, Apple is taking direct aim at the PC. Are we now really seeing the post-PC world we were promised?

The iPad Pro is a powerful tablet, and starting with iOS 10, Apple opened up the operating system and allowed non-native apps access to features like Siri.

As the iPad continues to grow in processing power and versatility, are we ready to ditch the PC? We'll look at a few areas where the iPad has a leg up on the PC world.

<Just For The Elderly>

Security

You might be surprised to see security top a list of reasons to go iPad over PC, but the iPad is actually quite secure when compared to a PC. It is almost impossible for an iPad to be infected by a virus. Viruses work by jumping from one app to the next, but the iPad's architecture puts a wall around each app, which prevents one piece of software from overwriting a portion of another application.

It is also difficult to get malware onto the iPad. Malware on a PC can do anything from recording all of the keys you press on your keyboard to allowing your entire PC to be taken over remotely. It often makes its way onto a PC by tricking the user into installing it. This is the advantage of the App Store. With Apple checking every piece of software, it is much more difficult for malware to find its way onto the App Store, and when it does, it is removed quickly.

The iPad also offers several tools to secure your data and the device itself. The Find My iPad feature allows you to track your iPad if it is lost or stolen, lock it remotely, and even wipe all of the data from it remotely. And as Apple opens up the Touch ID fingerprint sensor to more uses, you can secure your data with your fingerprint. While possible on a PC, this biometric lock is made much easier on the iPad.

Performance

The iPad Pro's processor is the rough equivalent of an Intel i5 processor, which is the mid-range processor offered by the chipmaker. This processor makes the iPad much faster than those bargain-basement laptops you see on sale at Best Buy and the equal to most PCs you will find on sale in any store. It is certainly possible to find a PC that tops an iPad in pure performance, but you may need to also top $1000 on the price tag and even then, you probably won't beat the iPad in real-world performance.

There's a big difference in having a processor that does great on benchmark tests and having a device that is snappy in the real world, as the Samsung Galaxy Note 7 found out when it went head-to-head against the iPhone 6S in a real-world showdown. While the two are relatively close in benchmark tests, the iPhone actually performed about twice as fast in real-world tests of opening apps and performing tasks.

Value

The iPad and a PC are actually quite similar in terms of the price tag you'll see at the store. You can get into one for as cheap as $270, but you are probably going to pay between $400 to $600 for something powerful enough to do more than browse the web and with a life expectancy of more than a year or two.

But the price doesn't stop with the initial purchase. One big thing that can drive costs up for a laptop or desktop is the software. A PC doesn't do a lot out of the box. It can browse the web, but if you want to play games, type a term paper or balance your budget with a spreadsheet, you will probably need to buy some software. And it isn't cheap. Most software on the PC will range between $10 and $50 or more, with the ever-popular Microsoft Office costing $99 a year — although the major office apps are free as Windows Store apps.

Versatility
Not only does the iPad pack in some software you won't find in comparable PCs, but it also has some added features you won't find. In addition to the Touch ID fingerprint sensor previously mentioned, the newest iPads have fairly good cameras. The 9.7-inch iPad Pro has a 12 MP camera that can compete with most smartphones. The bigger Pro and the iPad Air 2 both have an 8 MP back-facing camera, which can still take pretty good pictures. You can also purchase an iPad with 4G LTE capabilities, which is a nice benefit over your standard laptop.

The iPad is also more mobile than a laptop, which is one of its main selling points. This mobility isn't just about carrying it with you when you travel. The biggest selling point is how easy it is to carry around your house or sit with you on the couch.

You can get some of the same versatility with a Windows-based tablet, but when compared to a laptop or desktop PC, the iPad certainly has an advantage.

Simplicity
Sometimes, not enough is made of the simplicity of the iPad. One of the biggest reasons why a PC's performance degrades over time and it begins to crash more often is user error, including installing software that loads when you power up the PC, not doing a proper shutdown when powered off, and many other common mistakes that can eventually plague a PC.

The iPad doesn't experience these problems. While an iPad has a chance to become slower or experience strange bugs over time, these are generally cleared up by a simple reboot. The iPad doesn't allow apps to self-load at startup, so there is no slow degradation of performance, and because there is no on-off switch, a user can't power down an iPad without it running through a proper shutdown sequence.

This simplicity helps keep the iPad bug free and in good working order.

Child-Friendly
Touchscreens are definitely more child-friendly than a keyboard, but you can always buy a laptop or desktop with a touchscreen. The increased mobility of the iPad is also a great advantage, especially with smaller children. But it is the ease of putting restrictions on the iPad and the number of great iPad apps for kids that really set it apart.

<Just For The Elderly>

The iPad's parental restrictions allow you to control the type of apps, games, music, and movies your child is allowed to download and watch. These controls come with the familiar PG/PG-13/R ratings and the equivalent for games and apps. You can also easily disable the App Store and default apps like the Safari browser. Within minutes of setting up the iPad, you can disable unfettered access to the web, which is great if you want your kid to have access to a powerful device like the iPad but want to keep them away from all of the not-so-kid-friendly messages, photos and video on the web.

But it is the multitude of kid-friendly apps that really sets the iPad apart. There are tons of great educational apps like Endless Alphabet and Khan Academy combined with a number of fun games that are perfect for kids aged 2, 6, 12 or older. And as mentioned previously, these apps and games tend to be much cheaper on the iPad than on a PC.

Gaming
The iPad isn't going to be mistaken for an Xbox One or a PS4. And if you are willing to shell out well over $1000, a PC can be the ultimate game machine. But if you are in the category of people who love to play games but wouldn't consider yourself a "hardcore" gamer, the iPad is the ultimate portable gaming system. It has far more powerful graphics than your standard $400-$600 PC, with graphics roughly the same as an Xbox 360.

There are also a ton of great games on the iPad. Again, you aren't going to find Call of Duty or World of Warcraft, but at the same time, you won't be shelling out $60 a pop for your gaming habit. Even the biggest games tend to top out at $10 and often cost less than $5.

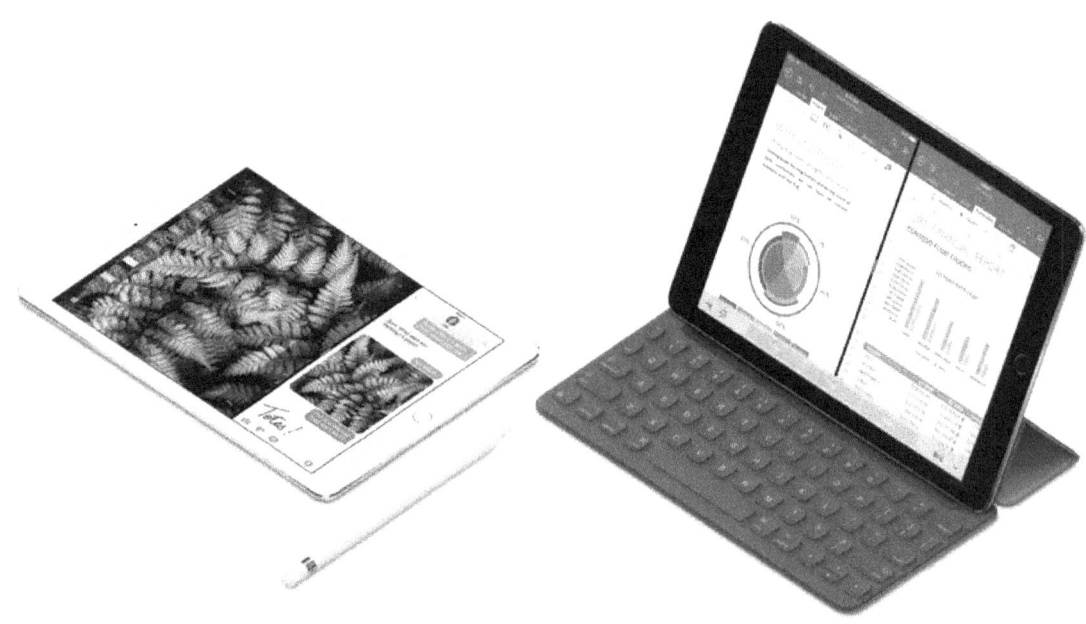

<Tom Carson>

Chapter 4: How To Send A Text Message

Sending a text message from your cell phone is one of the quickest and less intrusive ways of getting in touch with someone, but it's not a skill that everyone is born with. Here are steps for helping those new to text messaging.

Text Messaging Basics

Before we start, there are a few things to know about text messaging, also known as SMS (short message service), when just text is sent, or MMS (multimedia messaging service), which can include photos, audio, and other multimedia content:

You can send a text message to any modern cell phone even if you use a different wireless provider.
Each text message is limited to 160 characters, including spaces. If you try to send a message over 160 characters, your message will be split into several messages and delivered separately, right after each other.
Check your cell phone plan to see how much text messaging or texting costs. If you don't have a plan that includes texting, each message you send or receive will cost a small amount (around 0.20p per message, but more if you send a text message while roaming internationally or if you send an international text message).

How to Send a Text from Your Phone

Cell phones and smartphones will differ in the menu options and buttons, but in general, the process of sending a text message to someone else's phone is pretty straightforward.

From your phone's main menu find the "Messages" or "Messaging" option or application. Then select "Text Message" or "Text Messaging."

Illustration for article titled How to Send a Text Message
Choose "New Message" or "Write Message" or click on an icon that looks like it will create a new message (on my version of Android, it's a + sign; on the iPhone it's a square with a line, like a pen on paper).

enter in the phone number of the cell phone you want to send the message to. Many phones now let you select a contact from your phone's address book, so you could try typing in their name in the field to see if it will fill in the number for you. You can send a text message to more than one contact at a time on the iPhone and Android phones by clicking on the plus sign icon or continuing to enter contacts in the To: field.

<Just For The Elderly>

on the iPhone, click on the camera icon). This will bring up your options for sending a photo, video, etc.

type in your message in the message field and hit "Send".

Replying To and Forwarding Messages
If you get a text message from someone else, you can easily send them a reply by opening the message and typing in your response in the text box at the bottom.

To forward a text message, on Android phones and iPhone, tap and hold the message to forward then select the option to forward the message. On other cell phones, the option to forward will probably be under "options" or a similar menu. Enter the phone number to send the message to and click "Send".

That's pretty much all there is to it. If in doubt, your cell phone manual should have more precise directions for you

OR………..

Send a message
You can send a text message to one or more people.

Tap the Compose button at the top of the screen.

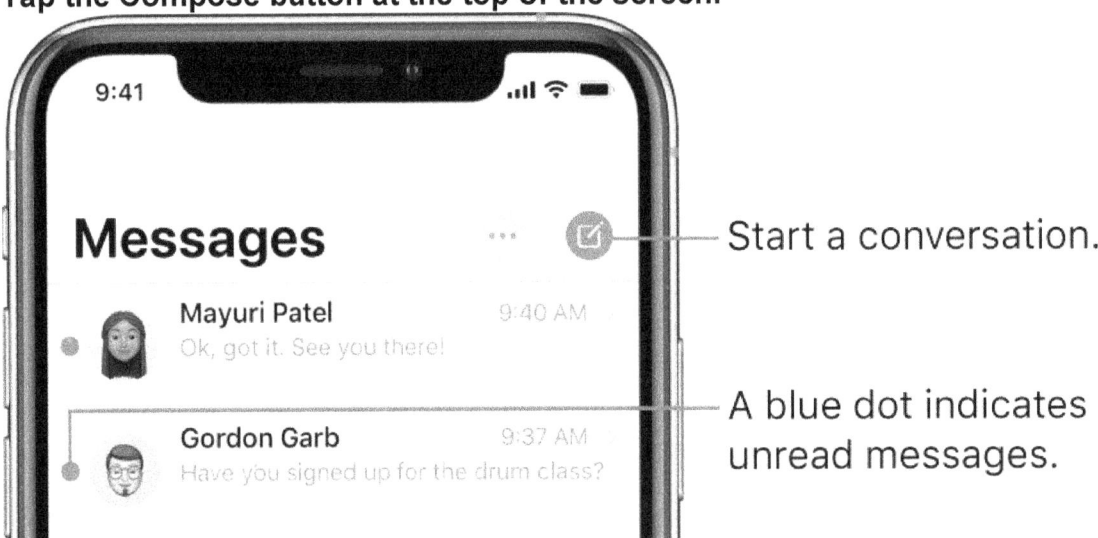

<Tom Carson>

Enter the phone number, contact name, or Apple ID of each recipient. Or, tap the Add button, then choose contacts.

On models with Dual SIM, to send an SMS/MMS message from a different line, tap the line shown, then choose the other line. See also Manage your cellular plans.

Tap the text field, type your message, then tap the Send button to send.

A blue send button indicates the message will be sent with iMessage; a green send button indicates the message will be sent with SMS/MMS, or your cellular service.

An alert Alert badge appears if a message can't be sent. Tap the alert to try sending the message again.

Tip: To see what time a message was sent or received, drag a bubble to the left

To view conversation details, tap the name or phone number at the top of the screen, then tap the More Info button. You can tap the contact to edit the contact card, share your location, view attachments, leave a group conversation, and more.

To return to the messages list from a conversation, tap the Back button or swipe from the left edge.

Reply to a message
Ask Siri. Say something like:

"Send a message to Eliza saying how about tomorrow"

"Reply that's great news"

"Read my last message from Bob"

Learn how to ask Siri

Tip: When you wear AirPods Pro, AirPods (2nd generation), or other supported headphones, Siri can read your incoming messages, and you can speak a reply for Siri to send (iOS 13.2 or later). See Listen and respond to messages.

Or do the following:

In the Messages list, tap the conversation that you want to reply to.

<Just For The Elderly>

To search for contacts and content in conversations, pull down the Messages list and enter what you're looking for in the search field. Or, choose from the suggested contacts, links, photos, and more.

Tap the text field, type your message, then tap the Send button to send.

Tip: To replace text with emoji, tap the Next Keyboard, Emoji button or the Next Keyboard button to switch to the Emoji keyboard, then tap each highlighted word.

You can quickly reply to a message with a Tapback, like a thumbs up or a heart. Double-tap the message bubble that you want to respond to, then choose your response.

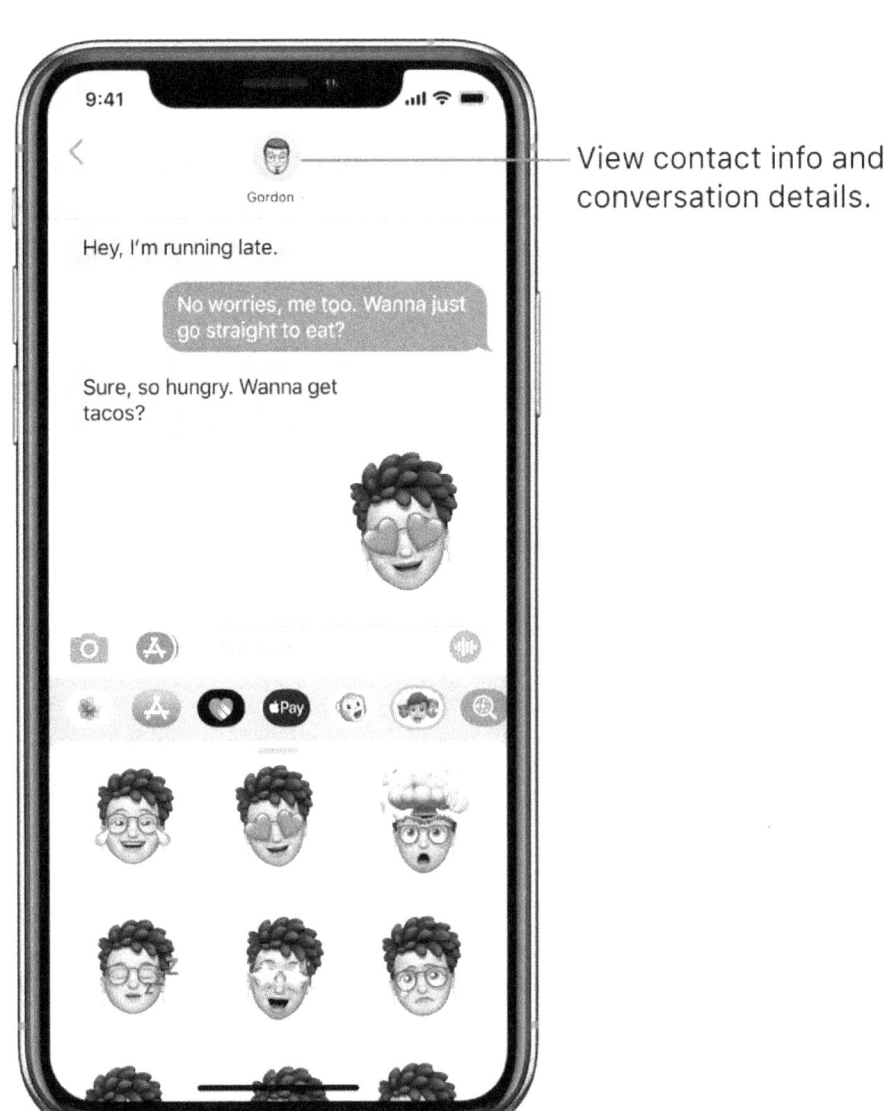

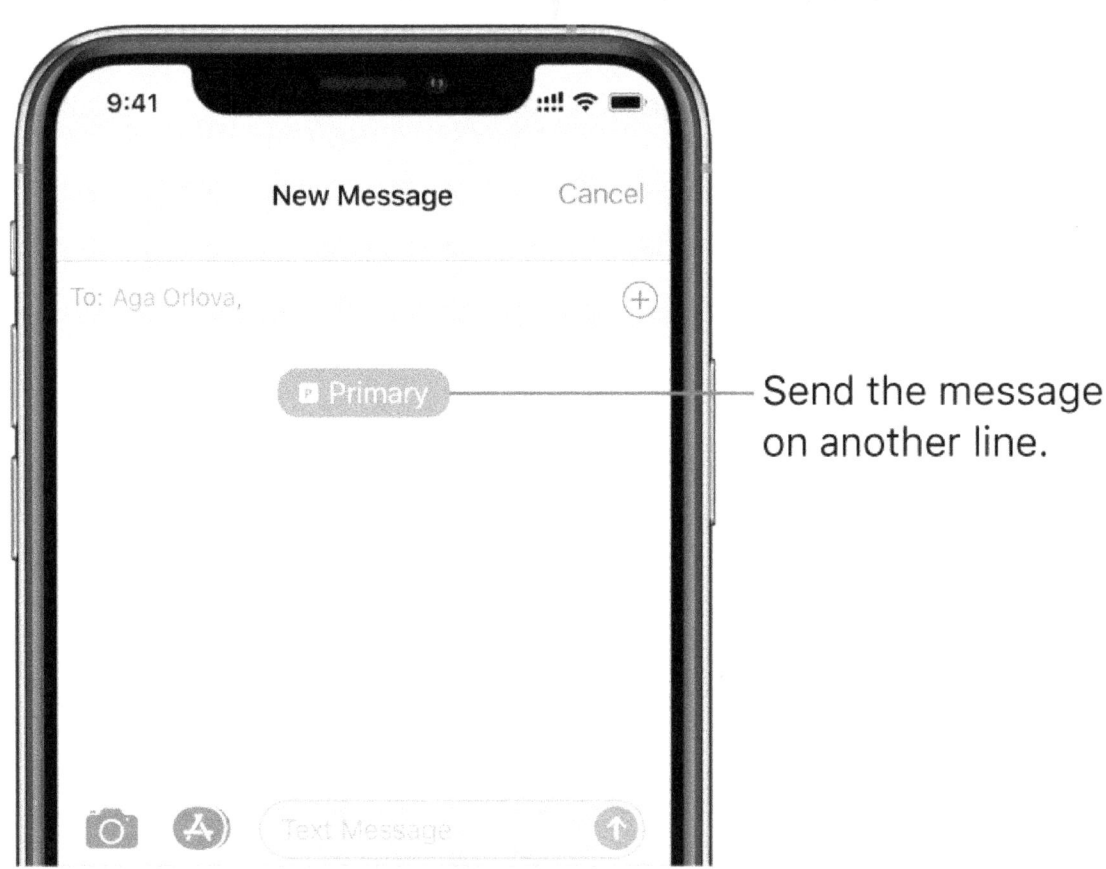

Send the message on another line.

In the Messages list, tap the Compose button.

The Messages list, with the Edit button at the top left and the Compose button at the top right. A blue dot to the left of a message indicates it's unread.
Enter the phone number or Apple ID of each recipient, or tap the Add button, then choose contacts.

On models with Dual SIM, to send an SMS/MMS message from a different line, tap the line shown, then choose the other line. See also Manage your cellular plans.

The Messages screen for a new SMS/MMS conversation. To send the message on your other line, tap the line button below the recipient.
Tap the text field, type your message, then tap the Send button to send it.

An alert Alert badge appears if a message can't be sent. Tap the alert to try sending the message again.

Tip: To see what time a message was sent or received, drag a bubble to the left.

<Just For The Elderly>

To view conversation details, tap the More Info button at the top of the screen. You can tap a contact to view the contact card, share your location, view attachments, leave a group conversation, and more.

To return to the messages list from a conversation, tap the Back button or swipe from the left edge.

Chapter 5: What Is A Boomer?

For a long time now, the cross-generational dialogue between baby boomers and millennials has been built atop several recurring themes. Boomers — the generation born roughly between 1946 and 1965 — scoff that millennials expect "participation trophies" for doing the bare minimum.

Millennials say boomers are "out of touch." Millennials (born roughly between 1980 and 1996) are "killing" once-stable industries like cereal by saving money, spending less, and "eating avocados." Boomers have "mortgaged the future" in exchange for hoarding wealth while also voting to end necessary social programs. Millennials would rather complain about student debt than buckle down, work hard, and "get a job."

If anything, teens have been subjected to even harsher rhetorical maligning. Members of Generation Z, born roughly between 1996 and 2015, are portrayed as addicted to their phones, "intolerant" of their elders, and stuck in a "different world" thanks to the internet.

With all this repetitive back-and-forth — seriously, there are bingo cards — it's no wonder the most polarizing meme of the year is a two-word dismissal of the whole debate. "OK boomer," which floated into the internet mainstream and rapidly gained traction this fall, is an attempt by millennials and Gen Z to both encapsulate this circular argument and reject it entirely.

OK boomer is meant to be cutting and dismissive. It suggests that the conversation around the anxieties and concerns of younger generations has become so exhausting and unproductive that the younger generations are collectively over it.

OK boomer implies that the older generation misunderstands millennial and Gen Z culture and politics so fundamentally that years of condescension and misrepresentation have led to this pointedly terse rebuttal and rejection. Rather than endlessly defend decisions stemming from deep economic strife, to save money instead of investing in stocks and retirement funds, to buy avocados instead of cereal — teens and younger adults are simply through.

<Just For The Elderly>

The conversation isn't through with them, however, not least because the rise of OK boomer has provoked concurrent backlash from baby boomers, many of whom have misread the meme, and feel it is motivated mainly by ageism. But that misreading also feeds the meme — because baby boomers failing to understand the point of OK boomer is, well, the point of OK boomer.

Don't get it twisted. It's important to understand that what really lies behind the meme is increasing economic, environmental, and social anxiety, and the feeling that baby boomers are leaving younger generations to clean up their mess.

BUT CUT ALL THE LONG DESCRIPTION HERE IT HIS ALL SUMMED UP

In early November 2019, a TikTok video was uploaded showing a grey-haired man - thought to be a Baby Boomer, (that's someone born between 1946 and 1964), saying "millennials and Generation Z have the Peter Pan syndrome."

It was his way of saying people born in this period don't want to grow up.

On a split screen next to him, a Gen Zer (that's someone born between 1995 to 2015) silently holds up a notepad, saying: "OK Boomer."

Since 14 November, the hashtag #OKBoomer has been used more than 732 million times, while more than 2,000 official hoodies bearing the catchphrase have been sold.

It started as a teenage comeback to basically any older person who's making fun of young people or seems out of touch about the issues that matter to them.

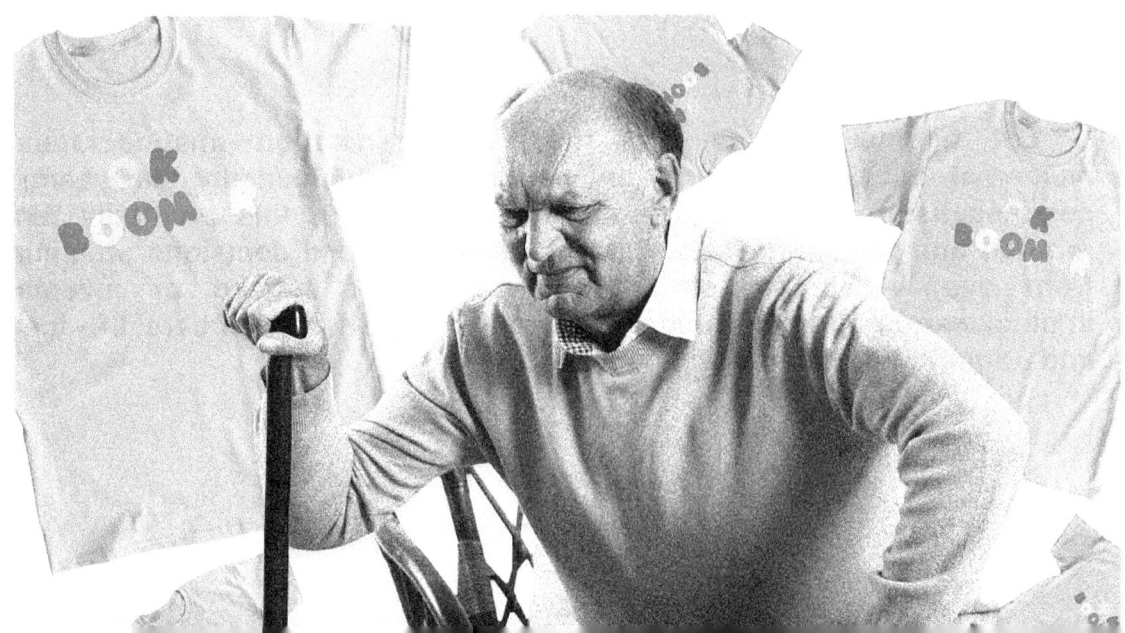

<Tom Carson>

In recent months, the phrase "OK boomer" has become a common retort in the parts of the internet inhabited by teenage and young adult users. On Instagram, the phrase appears as a hashtag alongside memes and artwork mocking the older generation. On Twitter, the phrase is hurled at someone for making an outdated statement. And on TikTok, where it is arguably the most prolific, it appears in artwork, audios and makeup tutorials as a way to mock an older generation, and the hashtag has been viewed on the platform 18 million times.

"I think a big part of why it has caught on is just, like, baby boomers and older people in general love to complain about younger people on the whole," said Sam Harman, 17, who took part in the "OK boomer" picture. "They'll call anyone younger than them 'millennials,' and doing the same thing to older people by calling them 'boomers' is kind of a push back to that."

The phrase is a culmination of annoyance and frustration at a generation young people perceive to be worsening issues like climate change, political polarization and economic hardship. The 10 teens and young adults who spoke to NBC News about the phrase said "OK boomer" marked a boiling point for Gen Z and younger millennials, who feel pushed around or condescended to by older generations.

The phrase is even being used to sell sweatshirts.

"I feel like it caught on so well because it's catchy and humorous, but it also got such a big reaction out of the older generation, which gave it its power essentially and caused people to use it more," Cassidy Carter, 19, said.

"They underestimate us a lot just because of our age and how we're growing up," Saptarshi Biswas, 17, said. "They think we're given everything, but I think another thing they don't realize is that they're making decisions for our future and they aren't really taking responsibility for it, and I think 'OK boomer' is kind of an accountability check."

But young people are split as to whether the term is akin to adults calling them "snowflake." Many say they feel "boomer" is an inoffensive way to brush off criticism from the older generation.

"I don't think 'OK boomer' is a retort on the 'snowflake' name-calling," said Hannah Hill, 20. "It isn't intended in the malicious way that 'snowflake' is

<Just For The Elderly>

aimed at younger generations. It's a funny way the younger people can laugh off the entitlement of some baby boomers. It is a humorous way to say 'OK, whatever' and move on with our lives."

The word also isn't exclusively lobbed at older people. Young people often use it against one another if they feel another person their age is being closed-minded or says something that sounds like it came from an older generation.

"Boomer can be applied more to personality than really what date you were born," said Nick Carver, 17.

Luca Brennan, who came up with the idea for the "OK boomer" picture for his senior panorama photo, agreed.

"A boomer is really more of a type of personality, someone who is intolerant to new ideas and who is ignorant to new ideas," Brennan said. "Stuff like that."

Tech

Although teens said they use it with condescending adults online and to tease one another, they said they also direct it at their parents when they feel they're being unfair or overly conservative.

"The one person I've called a boomer is my father. I think it describes him accurately because he's very stubborn and old-fashioned," Brennan said, adding that his father became defensive when the teen replied to criticisms with the phrase.

Brennan said when he was recently critiqued by his father for always being on his phone, he used the phrase "OK boomer," and then explained that older generations were responsible for things like "climate change, the 2008 financial crisis," and "several wars we should not have been in."

"Boomers come from a different era. They're behind the times. They're out of touch," Brennan said.

The rise of the phrase "OK boomer" mirrors the growing anger among young people at the older generation's passivity for the issues facing the world, not only today, but for the issues that young people say will be left to them to figure out once they become adults.

"I think of 'OK boomer' as kind of saying, you're a hypocrite," Carver said. "You're criticizing us for everything we're doing wrong when look at what you created of our world."

<Tom Carson >

Chapter 6: Why Is Apple Better Than Android

1. iPhones are faster

If you're thinking of buying a newer iPhone, know that the A12 Bionic chip inside beats anything from the Android camp. For example, the iPhone XS beat the Galaxy S10 Plus' Snapdragon 855 chip in Geekbench 4, which measures overall performance. The gap is narrower than it has been in the past, thanks to the Snapdragon 855 processor that will power this year's leading Android phones, but the iPhone XS scored a higher 11,420 to the 855-powered Galaxy S10 Plus' 10,732.

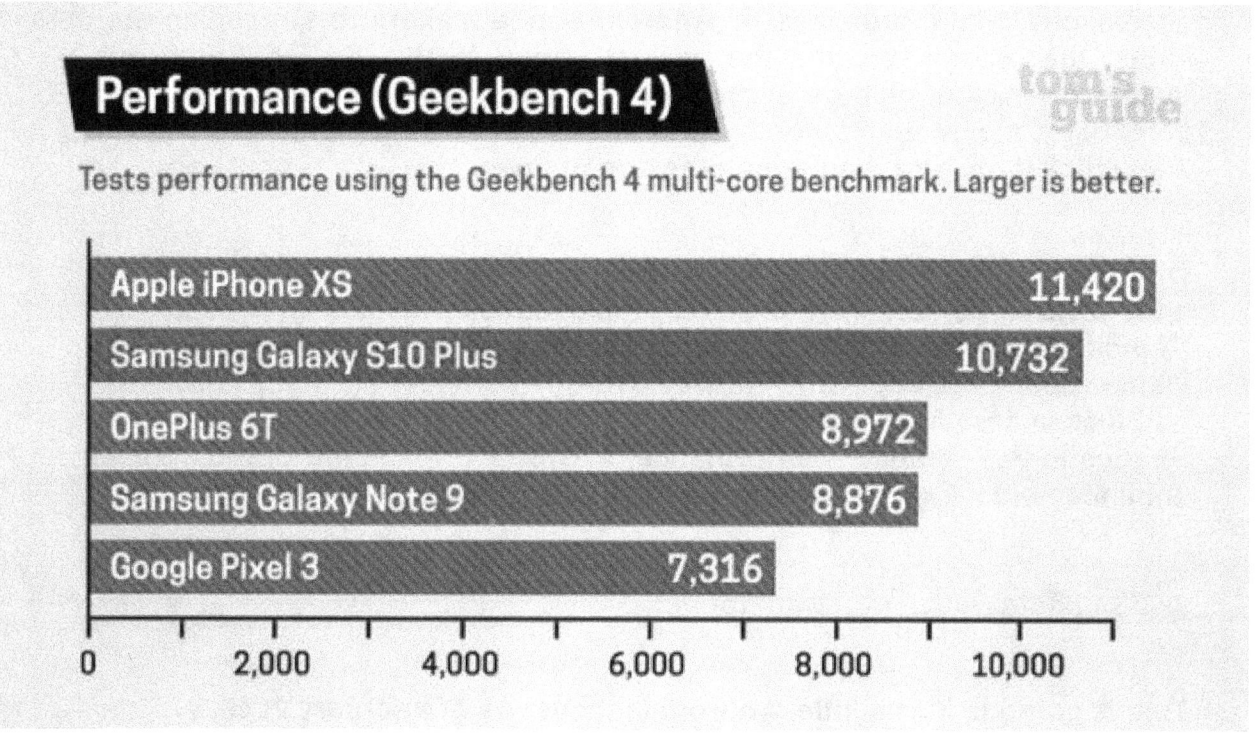

We've also found that the latest iPhones can transcode video faster in our editing test, with the iPhone XS taking just 39 seconds, compared to nearly 2.5 minutes for the Galaxy S10. This speed difference also makes enjoying demanding augmented-reality apps a smoother experience.

<Just For The Elderly>

2. Better hardware and software integration

Other the years, there's been plenty of examples of the advantage Apple has of owning the whole widget, which means that there's certain things that only it can pull off. Or at least pull off well before anyone else.

The latest example is Face ID, which securely logs you into the iPhone using a 3D scan of your face via a TrueDepth sensor. Other companies have attempted to copy Face ID, but none have succeeded.

Animoji and Memoji are other examples of Apple hardware and software working seamlessly together. Samsung's equivalent, AR Emoji, seems like a half-baked effort by comparison.

3. Easiest phone to use

Despite all the promises by Android phone makers to streamline their skins, the iPhone remains the easiest phone to use by far. Some may lament the lack of change in the look and feel of iOS over the years, but I consider it a plus that it works pretty much the same as it did way back in 2007. Pick it up, turn it on, touch the app to open.

Of course, Apple has folded in enhancements over the years, such as Siri and Control Center. Wth iOS 11, Apple added the ability to edit Live Photos, send payments to friends in the Messages app and organize files via a proper Files app (which is way overdue considering that Android has had files access from the start). And in iOS 12, users got Siri Shortcuts and Suggestions, faster performance, Group Facetime and other enhancements. Expect the improvements to continue with iOS 13 this fall.

4. OS updates when you want them

This is going to hurt a little, Android fanboys. As of February 2019, a whopping 83 percent of all iOS devices introduced in the last 4 years were using iOS 12, according to Apple. Google hasn't even published adoption rate numbers for the latest Android Pie as of April 2019. And it took about a year for the older Android Oreo to get to just 19 percent penetration.

The problem is this: With the exception of pure Android phones like the Pixel 3, the Samsng's and LG's of the world have to jump through more hoops to bring you the latest version of Google's OS. Plus, phone makers typically drag their feet on updating older phones. The situation is getting better, but not fast enough.If you own a compatible iPhone, you can update to the latest version of iOS on the day it's released (or close to it, depending on how Apple's servers stand up to the strain). This dynamic isn't going to change anytime soon.

5. The best apps first

Now that both iOS and Android have millions of apps in their stores, the arms race is over, right? Not really. The iPhone is still favoured by developers as the launch platform of choice for the hottest new apps.

The Google Play store is like the Netflix of app stores; it gets the hits, but usually after they see their first run on iOS. A prime example is Fortnite, which took several months to leap from iOS to Android, and even then it was a Samsung exclusive.

6. No bloatware!

Samsung and others have gotten better at minimizing the pain for users by lumping all carrier bloatware into a single folder, but it's still just crap taking up space on your phone.

You won't find a single piece of carrier software preloaded on an iPhone, making for a clean out-of-the-box experience. Apple does include some apps you might not want or need, like Apple Watch, but it has much more restraint than other manufacturers when it comes to bundling its own stuff.

7. Works beautifully with Macs

If you haven't tried a Mac in a while, you might be surprised to know just how well iPhones work with them. For instance, with the Continuity feature in macOS, you can use your MacBook to send and receive text messages and even receive and place calls. All you have to do is keep your iPhone nearby.

My favorite feature is AirDrop, which lets you easily transfer photos and videos over Wi-Fi from your iPhone to a MacBook. With macOS Mojave and iOS 12, the new Continuity Camera feature lets you instantly insert a photo into a document, mail or note.

And thanks to iCloud keeping everything in sync, you also have easy access on your Mac to the photos you take on your iPhone, as well as any notes or documents you create.

8. Apple Pay

Between Android Pay and Samsung Pay, Apple has plenty of rivals, but right now, Apple Pay is the most popular method for making mobile payments. It's also dead-simple to use. All you have to do to use Apple Pay is bring your iPhone close to the supported payment terminal at the checkout counter and then press your finger on your phone's Touch ID sensor. With the iPhone XS and iPhone XR, you just double tap the Side button and then stare at your phone to use Face ID.

If you're not that excited by using your phone to pay for stuff at the store, you can try another alternative: iOS supports sending and receiving money from friends and family from within the Messages app. Yes, there are third-party apps that do this, but with the iPhone, it's built right in.

9. Family Sharing

An Apple family that plays together saves together. With Family Sharing on the iPhone, Mom, Dad and the kids can share purchases from the App Store, iTunes and iBooks with up to six people. You can still keep your own iTunes accounts, too. When Junior wants to make a purchase, you receive an alert via the Ask to Buy feature, so you can keep better tabs on what he's downloading and also prevent bill shock.

10. Best support and help

When you have a problem with your Android phone, you can try finding a solution on online forums or calling your carrier. But with the iPhone, you can tap into a vast database of useful help articles on Apple's website, get help via live chat or schedule an appointment at an Apple Store Genius Bar.

<Just For The Elderly>

Chapter 7: How To Get Your Children Of The Phone

Talk may be cheap, but overage charges, not so much. Teens text over 3,000 times each month, according to the Nielsen Company. Even if you've got the best data overage plan on the planet, phone use, like all things in life, requires balance, and boundaries. Use these tricks to get your kids to look up from their phones, at least every now and then.

Teens are pretty universally tech-obsessed, but that doesn't mean you have zero say in the matter. "It's a parent's job to establish limits for the safe use of technology, so their kids can learn how to use communication devices in a healthy way," says Jamison Monroe, founder and CEO of Newport Academy, a mental health treatment program for teens.

"You own your child's phone. It's your property. As a parent, you're in charge of setting common sense limits on its use, just like you do around driving, drugs, and alcohol." What's more, In this era of cyberbullying and online stalking, this is a safety issue for many teens, he adds.

According to the *New York Times*, screen addiction is a serious condition, which may lead some kids to view the cyber world as real, and the real world as fake. This behavior may be intensified if parents allow double-digit hours of screen time, especially when kids are young.

Your child's phone is the key their social world. If you want to establish boundaries around its use, taking it away as a routine punishment for overuse is sure to backfire. As reported by the Child Mind Institute, virtual communication has a positive role in your child's life, and eliminating it entirely can damage trust. "Your child's cell phone is their main lifeline, and connection to their world," explains Dr. Newman. "Acknowledging this can help guide you when you're setting boundaries and establishing consequences," she adds.

For many families, a shared dinner is an oasis of hard-won together time, carved out between soccer practice, late nights at the office, evening meetings, and other obligations. Constant buzzing and heads downcast over phones can take away from the experience. "Growing up, if the phone rang during dinner we didn't answer it," says motivational speaker and single mom, Kristen Darcy. "Now, with all the chiming, ringing, dinging and vibrating going on, it's challenging to be in the moment with your children." When Darcy's text chimes during dinner, she leads by example and lets it wait, but not before showing her children what their behavior looked like. "I sat down to dinner with my phone in my face, and basically ignored my children," she explains of her experiment. "They were shocked. They got what I was doing, but it worked anyway." Her favorite response was from her daughter, who indignantly said, "That's not the way we act in this family."

<Just For The Elderly>

Ericka Sterns' seven kids range in age from small to how-did-they-get-that-big, and she is no stranger to technology use (and overuse) in the home. Sterns uses the OurPact parental control app, to control phone usage. "I can turn their phones off in a second if they aren't listening, plus schedule off-time during school, and at night," she explains. The app includes a downloadable contract that parents and kids sign, plus guidelines about how to create a balanced use of technology in the home. It includes an app blocker, and parental time lock. Carolyn Hawkinson-Pruett Osci, an artist and mother of two, uses a nanny program called Norton Family, which includes monitoring features and a time supervisor.

It's not easy dealing with kids when they hate you. This may come as a spoiler alert, but at some point, all kids hate their parents. That being said, you still have to stick to your guns, even when your kids are having a breakdown about phone boundaries. "Before we got our kids' cell phones, we had them sign an agreement about what is and isn't appropriate," says Lori Holden, a mom and open adoption advocate. "Sometimes, we also request that they be in the moment, and put down their phones. This doesn't mean there's no whining about it. I've been told I'm the worst parent ever, but I don't cave in."

Including your kids in the cell phone rule-making process can help keep the channels of communication open. Your children need a chance to explain some of their usage to you, so they feel heard. For example, your child may need his or her phone for an hour (or more) of group studying time each day. "Whatever your family rules are, have your teens and tweens help you determine them," Dr. Newman says. "They are more likely to follow the rules if they have a say in what they are." Don't miss the secret habits of happy families.

<Tom Carson>

"Kids practically come out of the womb on their phones," Monroe says. If all other efforts to control their cell use fails, give your child a "dumb" flip phone, the kind that lets them call and text but has no bells and whistles. "The privilege here is to get back their smart phone, once they learn how to stay within the boundaries you've set," Monroe says. "At the same time, organize family family activities that don't involve technology, such as hikes, parks, and museums, and enforce the no-phone for anyone rule."

Whether they're 8 or 18, getting kids to go to sleep at a normal hour can be an uphill climb, but it's exponentially tougher if they're in the middle of an epic snapchat dialogue, group text extravaganza, or Facebook messenger marathon. But since late-night gadget use has been shown to disrupt the sleep cycle, according to Mashable, it's a good idea to require kids to unplug about an hour before bed. It lets their bodies and brains unwind, enabling them to sleep better. Support everyone in the household to make a practice of powering down before sleep, and enforce this rule by removing the phones from each bedroom—including your own

Well There You Go…..

<Just For The Elderly>

Chapter 8: The Final Speech

This Has Probably Bored You, Sorry, Read This Over Again to Get All of The Information.

**Thanks for Reading,
Tom**

<Tom Carson>

BEFORE YOU GO U CAN WRITE ANY NOTES FOR THE NEXT FEW PAGES

<Just For The Elderly>

<Tom Carson >

<Just For The Elderly>

<Tom Carson >

<Just For The Elderly>

<Tom Carson >

<Just For The Elderly>

<Tom Carson >

<Just For The Elderly>

<Tom Carson >

<Just For The Elderly>

<Tom Carson>

<Just For The Elderly>

<Tom Carson >

<Just For The Elderly>

<Tom Carson>

<Just For The Elderly>

THERE YOU GO

www.ingramcontent.com/pod-product-compliance
Lightning Source LLC
Chambersburg PA
CBHW081559040426
42444CB00012B/3170